Make and Eat

Vegetarian Food

Susannah Blake

WAYLAND

First published in
2008 by Wayland

Wayland
338 Euston Road
London NW1 3BH

Wayland
Level 17/207 Kent Street
Sydney NSW 2000

Senior editor: Jennifer Schofield
Designer: Jane Hawkins
Photographer: Andy Crawford
Proofreader: Susie Brooks

The author and publisher would like to thank the following
models: Adam Menditta, Harriet Couch, Demi Mensah, Robert
Kilminster, Aneesa Qureshi, Kaine Zachary Levy, Emel Augustin.

CIP data
 Blake, Susannah
   Vegetarian food. - (Make & eat)
   1. Vegetarian cookery - Juvenile literature
   I. Title
   641.5'636

ISBN: 978 0 7502 5357 4

Printed in China

Wayland is a division of Hachette Children's Books,
an Hachette Livre UK company.

Note to parents and teachers:
The recipes in this book are designed
to be made by children. However, we
recommend adult supervision at all times
as the Publisher cannot be held
responsible for any injury caused while
making these recipes.

Contents

All about vegetarian food

A vegetarian is someone who does not eat meat, fish or animal products such as gelatine, which is made from animal bones. There are many reasons why people choose to be vegetarian. For some people, their religion does not allow them to eat meat. Other people feel it is wrong to eat meat. Some people just prefer to eat other things instead.

EATING PROTEIN

If you decide not to eat meat or fish, it is very important that you still eat protein. Protein helps you to grow and helps your body to repair itself. Meat and fish provide protein. If you cut them out of your diet, you must replace them with other protein foods. Good sources of vegetarian protein include milk, eggs, cheese, nuts, beans and other pulses such as chickpeas and tofu and quorn.

A BALANCED DIET

As well as eating protein-providing foods, you must eat other types of food to have a balanced diet. These include carbohydrates, dairy foods, fruit and vegetables. Carbohydrates are starchy foods such as potatoes, pasta, rice and bread. These foods give you energy.

Cheese and yogurt are dairy foods that contain calcium, which is important for strong bones and teeth. Fruit and vegetables contain vitamins and nutrients, which are important for maintaining a healthy body.

Carbohydrates should make up about one-third of what you eat every day. Fruit and vegetables should make up about one-third, too. The rest of your food should be protein, such as nuts, and dairy, such as cheese. You can eat some foods containing fat and sugar, but these foods are less good for you so it is best not to eat too many of them.

GET STARTED!

In this book you can learn to make all kinds of vegetarian food. All the recipes use everyday kitchen equipment, such as knives, spoons, forks and chopping boards. You can see pictures of the different equipment that you may need on page 23. Before you start, check that you have all the equipment that you will need and make a list of any ingredients that you need to buy. Make sure there is an adult to help you, especially with the recipes that involve using the cooker or oven.

When you have everything you need, make sure all the kitchen surfaces are clean and wash your hands well with soap and water. If you have long hair, tie it back. Always wash raw fruit and vegetables under cold running water before preparing or cooking them. This will help to remove any dirt and germs. Then, put on an apron and get cooking!

Tasty hummus

This creamy dip is packed with protein and makes a great snack. If you do not have a food processor, you can use a potato masher instead. Simply put all the ingredients in a bowl and mash until smooth.

INGREDIENTS

For 4 servings:
• 400g can chickpeas, rinsed
• 1 garlic clove, peeled • 1 tsp ground cumin
• 1 tsp ground coriander • 4 tbsp olive oil
• 1 tbsp tahini • 2 tbsp lemon juice
• salt and ground black pepper
• 3 carrots, peeled • 2 pitta breads

EXTRA EQUIPMENT

• food processor • toaster

1 Put the chickpeas in a food processor. If you have a hand-held food processor, put them in a large bowl.

2 Slice the garlic finely and add it to the chickpeas.

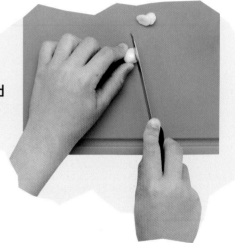

3 Add the cumin, coriander, olive oil, tahini and lemon juice to the chickpeas. Add a pinch of salt and a grinding of black pepper.

4 Blend all the ingredients together until the mixture is smooth. If necessary, turn off the food processor part of the way through, scrape down the sides of the bowl or food processor using a spatula, then blend again.

5 Taste the hummus and add more salt and black pepper if necessary. If the hummus is very thick, add a teaspoon of water and blend again until smooth. Spoon the hummus into a serving bowl.

6 Cut off the ends of each carrot. Cut the carrots in half lengthways then lay the halves on their flat sides and cut into sticks. Put the carrot sticks into another serving dish.

7 Toast the pitta breads until they are golden. When they are cool, cut them into fingers.

8 Put the pitta fingers in a dish and serve with the hummus and carrot sticks.

TAHINI

Tahini is a creamy paste made of ground sesame seeds that is used in Middle Eastern dips. It has a savoury, nutty taste and helps to give hummus its distinctive flavour.

Tricolore salad

This is a traditional salad that you will find on the menu in Italian restaurants. Tricolore, which is pronounced 'tree-co-lor-ay', means three colours. The name reflects the three colours of the salad: red tomato, green avocado and white mozzarella. These are also the colours of the Italian flag.

INGREDIENTS

For 4 servings:
- 2 tomatoes
- 1 ball of mozzarella (about 150g)
- 1 avocado
- 2 tsp red wine vinegar
- small pinch of sugar
- 5 tsp extra virgin olive oil
- salt and black pepper

1 Put four plates on your work surface. Cut the tomatoes into slices about 6mm thick. Arrange a quarter of the slices on each serving plate.

2 Cut the mozzarella ball in half and then cut each half into slices about 6mm thick. Arrange a quarter of the slices on each plate with the tomatoes.

3 Cut into the avocado lengthways, all the way down to the stone, then all the way round the stone. Holding half the avocado in each hand, twist the halves in opposite directions so that they come apart.

4 Ask an adult to help you remove the stone from the avocado.

5 Cut each avocado half in half again and peel off the skin. Cut the avocado into slices about 6mm thick. Arrange a quarter of the slices on each plate with the tomato and mozzarella.

6 To make the dressing, whisk the vinegar, sugar and olive oil together and season it with a pinch of salt and a grinding of black pepper. Drizzle the dressing over the salads and serve straight away.

KEEPING THEM GREEN!

When some fruits, such as apples and avocados, are cut, their flesh turns brown because it reacts with the oxygen in air. It does not make the fruit harmful to eat but it does not look nice. This is why you should serve this salad as soon as you have made it.

Scrambled eggs

Eggs are a good source of protein. You can eat scrambled eggs for breakfast, lunch or dinner, but if you want to serve them as a main meal, you should have them with vegetables or a side salad.

INGREDIENTS

For 1 serving:
- 2 eggs
- salt and black pepper
- 2 slices bread
- a knob of butter, plus extra for spreading on the toast

EXTRA EQUIPMENT
- toaster

Ask an adult to help you use the cooker.

1 Follow the instructions in the panel to crack the eggs into a bowl. Then, add a pinch of salt and a grinding of black pepper and beat them together with a fork.

2 Put the bread in a toaster to toast.

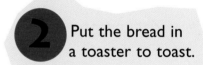

HOW TO CRACK AN EGG

1. Hold the egg in one hand and knock the middle on the side of a bowl to make a deep crack in its shell.

2. Holding the egg over the bowl, put your thumbs into the crack.

3. Pull the halves apart so that the egg falls into the bowl. Check that no bits of shell fell into the bowl.

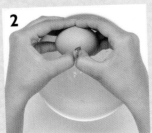

3 Put a non-stick pan over a medium heat and melt the knob of butter. When the butter sizzles, pour in the eggs. Stir the eggs with a wooden spatula, scraping it across the bottom of the pan to break up the egg as it sets.

4 When the eggs are set but still moist, take the pan off the heat. The eggs will continue cooking, so it is important that they are still moist and not completely cooked when you take the pan off the heat.

5 When the toast is ready, put it on a plate and spread it with butter.

6 Give the eggs a stir, then spoon them onto the toast. Grind over a little more black pepper and they are ready to eat.

Tofu kebabs

These healthy skewers make a tasty lunch or supper dish. Once you have mastered this recipe, you could try using courgettes and orange peppers instead of the tomatoes and yellow pepper.

INGREDIENTS

For 4 servings:
- 1 yellow pepper
- 1 red onion, peeled
- 300g firm tofu
- 150g cherry tomatoes
- 2 tbsp hoi sin sauce
- 1 tsp soy sauce
- 2 tsp sunflower oil
- 1 tsp lime juice

EXTRA EQUIPMENT

- 8 wooden skewers
- kitchen towel
- aluminium foil

Ask an adult to help you use the grill.

1 Soak the skewers in water while you make the rest of the recipe. This will stop the sticks from burning when they are under the grill.

2 Cut the pepper in half lengthways through the green stalk. Pull the two halves apart, then cut around the stalk and throw it away. Pull out the seeds and white pith and throw that away, too. Cut each half into quarters and then into chunks. Set aside the chunks for later.

3 Place the onion upright on the board and cut it in half. Put each half on its flat side and cut each one into quarters. Divide each quarter into layers and set them aside to use later.

4 Cut the tofu into 2cm cubes. Set them aside for later.

5 Dry the skewers on a clean kitchen towel.

6 Thread layers of pepper, onion, tofu and tomato onto the skewers.

7 To make the marinade, put the hoi sin sauce, soy sauce, sunflower oil and lime juice in the small bowl and mix them together.

8 Turn on the grill. If you are using an electric grill, leave it to heat up for about 5 minutes. In the meantime, line the grill pan with aluminium foil and arrange the skewers on top.

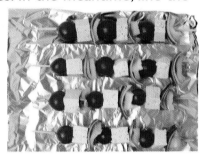

9 Brush about half the marinade onto the skewers and grill them for about 5 minutes. Turn the skewers over and brush them with more marinade. Grill for another 3 minutes until they are golden and ready to eat. Why not try them with some rice or pasta salad?

TOFU

Tofu is made from soya beans. The beans are soaked in water, then ground and boiled with water. This mixture is strained to make a white liquid. Things are added to the liquid so that it 'sticks together' to become more solid – a bit like cheese. The cheese-like mixture is then pressed to squeeze out the liquid. The end result is firm, white tofu.

Couscous salad

Couscous is a carbohydrate made from wheat. It looks like a grain and has a slightly nutty flavour. The butter beans in this salad are packed with protein and the peppers and tomatoes are full of vitamins and minerals.

INGREDIENTS

For 4 servings:
- 1 yellow pepper
- 250g cherry tomatoes
- 15g bunch basil
- 200g couscous
- 250ml water
- 1 tbsp lemon juice
- 2 tbsp olive oil
- ½ tsp clear honey
- 400g can butter beans
- salt and black pepper

EXTRA EQUIPMENT

- kettle

Ask an adult to help you use the kettle.

1 Cut the pepper in half lengthways through the green stalk. Pull the two halves apart, then cut around the stalk and throw it away. Pull out the seeds and white pith and throw them away. Cut the flesh into bite-sized pieces, about 2cm square, and put them into a small bowl.

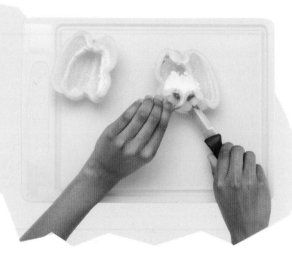

2 Cut each tomato in half and add them to the peppers.

IN THE WASH

It is important to wash vegetables and fruit before you eat or cook them. Fruit and vegetables grown with the help of fertilisers and pesticides may still have chemicals on them, which could harm your body. Organic fruit and vegetables will not have chemicals on them but they may be dirty, so wash them, too.

14

3 Pull the basil leaves from the stalks and throw the stalks away. Gently tear the leaves into little pieces and add them to the bowl with the tomatoes and peppers.

4 Boil the water in a kettle. Put the couscous in a large bowl and sprinkle over a pinch of salt. When the water has boiled, pour it over the couscous.

5 Leave the couscous to stand for 5 minutes until it has soaked up all the water. Run a fork through it to separate the grains.

6 To make the dressing, put the lemon juice, olive oil and honey in a bowl and add a pinch of salt and a grinding of black pepper. Whisk it all together until it is mixed.

7 Add the beans, peppers, tomatoes and basil to the couscous and pour over the dressing.

8 Using two large spoons, fold the ingredients together. Start with the spoons at the bottom on the bowl and slowly bring them to the top, stirring the ingredients together as you go. When the salad is well mixed, spoon it into four bowls to serve.

Minestrone soup

Minestrone is a classic Italian pasta soup. This recipe suggests using vermicelli pasta but you can use other pasta shapes that are made especially for soups.

INGREDIENTS

For 4 servings:
- 1 onion, peeled
- 2 garlic cloves
- 2 tbsp olive oil
- 400g can chopped tomatoes
- 1 tbsp sun-dried tomato puree
- 1.2 litres vegetable stock
- 1 carrot
- 115g green beans
- 60g vermicelli
- ground black pepper

Ask an adult to help you use the cooker.

1 Cut the onion in half and then chop each half finely. Set aside for later.

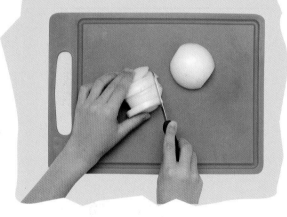

2 Peel the garlic cloves. Put each clove in a garlic press to crush it.

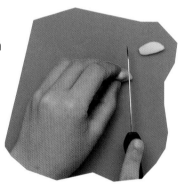

3 Heat the oil in a saucepan over a medium heat. Add the onion and garlic and fry for 4 minutes.

WATERY EYES

Onions contain natural chemicals called allicins. When you cut up onions, you release these chemicals and when the allicins react with your eyes, they can make them sting and water.

16

4 Add the tomatoes, tomato puree and stock. Bring to the boil, then turn the heat to low and cover the saucepan with a lid. Simmer for 15 minutes.

5 While the soup simmers, peel the carrot. Cut off both ends, then cut the carrot in half lengthways and in half again. Slice the quartered carrots thinly and set them aside to use later.

6 Cut off the very end of each bean and then slice each bean into 1-cm lengths. Set aside to use later.

7 When the soup has been simmering for 15 minutes, carefully take off the lid and add the carrots and beans. Put the lid back on and let the soup simmer for a further 5 minutes.

8 Add the pasta and simmer for 2 minutes more until the pasta is tender. Season with black pepper, then ladle the soup into bowls to serve.

Jacket potato with chilli beans

You can make the chilli beans as spicy hot as you like. If you like things extra hot, add a pinch more chilli, or if you do not like things hot at all, leave out the chilli and add black pepper instead.

1 Preheat the oven to 190°C/375°F/Gas 5. Prick the potatoes all over. Rub a little oil over each potato and sprinkle with salt.

2 Bake the potatoes for about 1 hour until they are crisp on the outside and soft in the middle. To test whether a potato is cooked, put a knife into the potato. It should feel soft all the way through.

3 While the potatoes bake, make the chilli. Put the onion on a chopping board and slice off both ends. Slit the brown skin and peel it off, then chop the onion finely.

4 Use a garlic press to crush the garlic.

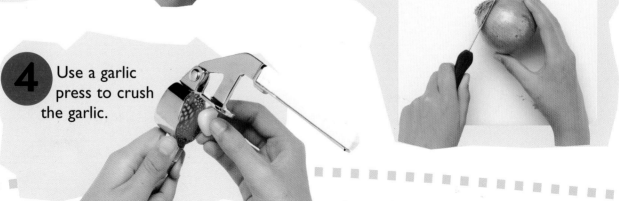

5 Heat the olive oil in a pan over a medium heat. Fry the onion and garlic for 5 minutes.

6 Add the beans along with the tomatoes, tomato puree, cumin and chilli to the saucepan. Let the mixture boil, then reduce the heat to low and cover the saucepan with a lid. Simmer for 25 minutes, stirring occasionally, then turn off the heat.

7 When the potatoes are cooked, warm through the chilli again if it is not hot enough.

8 Add a knob of butter to each potato, then top with some chilli and plain yogurt.

9 Wearing oven gloves, put each potato on a plate. Cut a deep cross in the top of each potato to open it.

POTATO TUBERS

If farmers left potatoes underground, roots and stems would grow from them into a new plant. The part of the potato plant that we eat is called a tuber.

Chunky pasta

Timing is important when you cook pasta dishes. You should aim for the pasta and sauce to be ready at the same time so that everything is perfectly cooked.

INGREDIENTS

For 4 servings:
- 150g mushrooms
- 1 large courgette
- 2 garlic cloves, peeled
- 2 tbsp olive oil
- 400g can chopped tomatoes
- ¼ tsp dried oregano
- salt and ground black pepper
- 300g dried penne or other pasta shapes
- grated cheese

Ask an adult to help you use the cooker.

1 Cut the mushrooms into slices about 6mm thick and set them aside for later.

2 Put the courgette onto a board and cut off both ends. Slice the courgette in half lengthways and then place each half on the board, cut side down. Cut each half lengthways into three long strips. Cut each strip into chunks. Set them aside.

3 Crush each garlic clove in a garlic press.

4 To make the sauce, heat the oil over a medium heat. Add the garlic and fry it for about 1 minute – be careful not to let it burn.

5 Add the mushrooms and fry gently for 5 minutes, stirring occasionally. Add the tomatoes and oregano and season the mixture with a pinch of salt and black pepper. Bring the sauce to the boil, then turn the heat to low. Simmer the sauce for 10 minutes.

6 Add the courgettes and a pinch more salt. Stir the sauce then let it simmer for about 15 minutes, stirring occasionally, until the courgettes are tender but not completely soft.

7 While the courgettes cook, cook the pasta by following the instructions on the packet. When the pasta is cooked, drain it and add it to the sauce. Mix it all together and spoon it into serving bowls. Spinkle on some grated cheese before you serve the pasta.

PASTA

There are hundreds of different types of pasta. Long pasta includes spaghetti and vermicelli; short pasta includes penne. Ravioli is a popular stuffed pasta and lasagne is a flat pasta that is baked in the oven.

Glossary

balanced diet

This means eating carbohydrates, protein, fat, vitamins, minerals and fibre in the correct proportions to allow your body to work properly.

calcium

This important mineral found in dairy foods strengthens your bones and teeth.

carbohydrates

Found in starchy foods, such as potatoes, bread, pasta and rice, carbohydrates provide your body with the energy it needs to work every day.

gelatine

A clear, tasteless substance used to make jellies.

knob of butter

A small amount of butter. If you had to weigh a knob of butter, it would be about 8g.

marinade

A sauce used to flavour food. Often food is soaked in the marinade before it is cooked.

Middle East

The countries to the east of the Mediterranean Sea from Egypt to Iran.

nutrients

The goodness found in food that our bodies need to survive.

protein

Found in meat, fish, eggs, dairy foods, nuts, seeds, pulses, tofu and quorn, protein helps to build muscle and keep other organs inside your body healthy.

pulses

Peas, lentils and beans.

quorn

A type of vegetarian protein.

simmer

When a liquid boils, the surface bubbles rapidly but when you turn down the heat, and the surface moves very gently, this is called simmering.

tubers

The swollen part of an underground root. Potatoes are probably the best-known of all tubers.

vitamins

The nutrients that your body needs to grow and develop normally.

EXTRA INFORMATION

These abbreviations have been used:
- tbsp – tablespoon • tsp – teaspoon
- ml – millilitre • g – gram • l – litre

To work out where the cooker dial needs to be for high, medium and low heat, count the marks on the dial and divide it by three. The top few are high and the bottom few are low. The in-between ones are medium.

Equipment

PASTRY BRUSH
Use to brush marinades and oil onto foods.

LADLE
Scoop soup into bowls using a ladle.

COLANDER
Use colanders over the sink, either for washing fruit and vegetables or for draining pasta and cooked vegetables.

GARLIC PRESS
Crush garlic finely by putting a peeled garlic clove inside the press and squeezing the handle.

MEASURING SPOONS
Measuring spoons help you to use the exact amount of ingredients.

CHOPPING BOARDS
These protect your work surface. Make sure you keep your chopping boards clean and always use a different one for meat and vegetables.

PLASTIC SPATULA
These are great for scraping mixtures such as dips from the sides of bowls.

KNIVES
Be careful when chopping and always keep your fingers away from the sharp blade.

WOODEN SPOONS AND SPATULAS
Use these to stir food when cooking. Flat-ended spatulas are good for scraping foods such as scrambled eggs from the bottom of a pan.

FRYING PAN
Use this flat pan to fry vegetables or eggs. You will need to add very little butter or oil to a non-stick pan.

BOX GRATER
Use to grate food such as cheese and carrots. Keep your fingers away from the sharp teeth of the grater.

Index